The Little Roads of Irel

Text and photos by

David Rice

RED STAG

Published in 2019
RED STAG
(a Mentor Books imprint)
Mentor Books Ltd
43 Furze Road
Sandyford Industrial Estate
Dublin 18
Republic of Ireland

Tel: +353 1 295 2112/3
Fax: +353 1 295 2114
email: admin@mentorbooks.ie
website: www.mentorbooks.ie

A CIP catalogue record for this title is available
from the British Library.

ISBN 978-1-912514-58-8

Contents

By the same author

Fiction

Blood Guilt
The Pompeii Syndrome
La Sindrome di Pompei
Song of Tiananmen Square
I Will Not Serve
Corduroy Boy

Non-fiction

Shattered Vows
The Dragon's Brood
Kirche ohne Priester
The Rathmines Stylebook
Yes, You Can Write
The Joy of Looking

About the author

A native of Northern Ireland, David Rice has worked as a journalist on three continents. He has also been a Dominican friar. He began his photography at age 16 while a student at Clongowes Wood College. In the 1970s he was a photo-journalist in the United States, where he worked also as an editor and Sigma-Delta-Chi award-winning syndicated columnist, returning to Ireland in 1980 to direct the Rathmines School of Journalism (later DIT). In 1989 he was invited to Beijing by London's Thomson Foundation, to train journalists on behalf of Xin Hua, the Chinese government news agency, and to work as an editor with China Features. He was in Beijing during the massacre of Tiananmen Square, and later returned to interview secretly 400 of the young people who had survived the massacre. This resulted in the unfortunate attention of the Chinese security police. His photos from the Tiananmen Square protest were published by HarperCollins in *The Dragon's Brood*. His later novel, *Song of Tiananmen Square* (Brandon/Mt Eagle), tells the full story of the massacre. Rice's 10 books have been published in Britain, Ireland, Germany, Italy and the United States. His No.1 best-selling *Shattered Vows* (Michael Joseph/Penguin; William Morrow, NY; C. Bertelsmann, Germany; Goldmann Verlag, Germany) led to the acclaimed YTV/Channel 4 documentary, *Priests of Passion*, which he presented. He now lives in Co Tipperary, has taught Writing Skills at the University of Limerick, and for 18 years directed the highly successful Killaloe Hedge-School of Writing, with visitors from 19 countries, and the publication of more than 100 books. The pictures in this present volume are selected from 170,000 of the author's photos. ■

For
Catherine Thorne
(Kathleen to me)
my companion
in all things

Acknowledgements

First I must mention the late Danny McCarthy who, as CEO of Mentor/Red Stag, asked me to do this book. May he rest in peace. His enthusiasm back then has kept me going during the last several years which it has taken me to finish this. But in fact one could say the book has taken more than three decades, as that's how long I have been taking photos of Irish roads and landscapes. When it came to actually creating the book, I had to learn a completely new software—*Adobe InDesign*—as used by my publisher, so that I could create the pages and place the pictures where they needed to go. I am deeply grateful to Kathryn O'Sullivan of Mentor/Red Stag, who helped me so much in my struggle to master InDesign, even linking our computers so as to demonstrate or solve a problem. Then there is Sean McDonagh—a computer guru who helped me so much in technical matters, and came up with some brilliant shortcuts. I must also thank Eugene McDonagh for his computer guidance, and the Killaloe Writers' Group who had to suffer my endless readings of bits of text and my showing of pictures. My sincere thanks too to editor and proof-reader Joan Lonergan, her of the eagle eye, who let nothing pass that shouldn't. And finally, I must thank my partner Kathleen, whom I must have bored to extinction, endlessly asking her advice on pictures and text. Her second name is patience. She'll go to heaven just for that.

—*David Rice*
November 2019

Foreword

The author gathers together a collection of images of a quiet Ireland. A rural landscape we are so used to seeing that we often don't stop to marvel at its beauty. Visitors from overseas will instantly see the verdant greens and vibrant colours of our countryside, but often, for the natives, we don't stop to enjoy it.

Perhaps with this collection the author can help you to take a moment the next time you find yourself on the little roads of Ireland.

As an artist, and more especially a landscape painter, I am conscious of the remarkably wide and various images of our countryside as shown in the illustrations in this book. The use of country roads conveys not only the look of these roadways, but their wider reference as the familiar landscape of the land itself. Most of us remember what they were like, more especially in our childhood memories. On a more mundane level, the plenitude of the illustrations prompts the question, how long was the photographer at work? My guess would be a lifetime. I know of no other collection, so particularised. Perhaps the tourist promoters will realise the usefulness of the book as a unique revelation of this other Ireland.

Thomas Ryan
Royal Hibernian Academy

The roads to God-knows-where

VERMEER's *Girl with the Pearl Earring* depicts a face of extraordinary beauty, with all its lineaments, eyes, nose, chin, in perfect harmony. But if you move in close to the canvas you see hundreds of tiny cracks where the paint has shrunk over the centuries.

Now look at an ordinance map of Ireland. You see the towns, the mountain ranges, the rivers, the harbours and the superb modern motorways. But move in close and you see hundreds of tiny cracks on the map.

Those cracks are the little roads of Ireland. They are quite simply the roads to God-knows-where, and many of them have been there since prehistoric times.

But it's where they can lead you is their magic. These little roads wind among the hills, up and down dales, taking you to places where few tourists ever venture, nor even our own Irish city dwellers. Yet many a turn can reveal an exquisite panorama of mountain or lake or farmland or sky, with those magnificent cumulus clouds so beloved of Paul Henry.

In the years when I lived and worked in the US and China, I used to dream of the little Irish roads I walked in my youth. So when I returned to Ireland

more than three decades ago, I began exploring these little roads with a camera, trying to capture their amazing visual beauty. Rarely just the roads themselves, but what you see through gateways into fields, or light filtering through trees along a forest road—what the Japanese call *komorebi*—or light dancing on a lake

at evening, or light caressing clouds high above the road.

Indeed it is all about light—what light can do to these little roads from one season to another. However I have called this book *The Little Roads of Ireland* simply because they are the ribbons that tie together these incomparable landscapes, so little >>

The roads to God-knows-where

known except by the folk who live there. Without these roads we would never get to see the Hidden Ireland.

The origins of these little roads are varied. Since Ireland was never part of the Roman Empire, the stone-paved roman roads were never here. In past centuries, apart from the five principal highways *(slighe)* there were side roads *(tógraite)*, which were sometimes tolled, and cow roads—essentially tracks made by cows, or for cows.

Hence the Gaelic name for a road—*bóthar*, which comes from the word *bó* —a cow. So *bóthar* actually means a cow track often from prehistoric times.

And then there were butter roads, to facilitate bringing farmers' butter to Cork, which supplied the whole British Empire. There were also the military roads, to get soldiers quickly into remote areas, so as to subdue rebellious populations.

And finally the pilgrim roads, to bring people to places that were sacred even in the time of the druids and are now sacred to christians.

Boreen *(bóithrín)* is simply the diminutive— meaning 'little road'. There are lots of other words for these roads, like track, lane, laneway, pathway.

And in Ulster they have the word *lonan*. It's always of course 'a wee lonan'.

Follow the Old Road, by Jo Kerrigan, is one of the loveliest and most informative books I have ever read about the little Irish roads. Her advice is clear: 'The amount you miss by following the main through route is incalculable. If you want to know more about the real Ireland, then do yourself a favour. Find the old road. Rediscover the old ways of travelling.

By turning off the main highway and discovering venerable routes, some of which have been travelled for thousands of years, you will see Ireland in an entirely different way.'

This present picture book tries to do just that— to show you Ireland in a different way. I can only show a tiny fraction of what I have encountered. But I want you to see textures and patterns and reflections along the roads.

want you to peep through gateways, which can sometimes be windows into considerable beauty.

Some roads can bring a sense of peace; some can reveal sad things, like memorials to accidents by the wayside. And the famine roads still seem to exude grief. Indeed why not?

Roads themselves vary wonderfully—from those with grass up the middle, to roads that are tunnels through trees, to roads that wind like serpents. And where the little roads end, by lake, river or mountain, or often by the sea, can often be dramatic. And sometimes dangerous.

There are 43 National Waymarked Trails in 25 counties, and National Geographic says Ireland is in the top five hiking destinations in the world. Details and maps can be got from *irishtrails.ie.*

A confession to make—at times I was careless in noting the exact spot where I took a photo, so sometimes I have had to guess when writing the caption. I would be glad to be corrected for any error. I have also used a few extracts of text from my book, *The Joy of Looking,* simply because I couldn't think of any better way to say it.

On these pages you won't see the Cliffs of Moher or the Giant's Causeway. There are quite enough pictures of such wonderful places. The pictures here are of the Hidden Ireland.

But please don't just look through them and leave it at that. Get out onto the little roads and explore for yourself. You never know what you might encounter.

One thing is certain, however—*you'll always meet a doggie.* They are the denizens of the little roads. They come trotting out of farmyard gates, mostly wagging their tails in friendship. And if one is not friendly, just raise your arm with an imaginary stick, take a step forward and the doggie will run yelping back through the gateway. Remember, all bullies are cowards. So, to acknowledge the doggies of the little roads, you are going to meet them throughout these pages too. *Slán.* ∎

Whatever else...

You'll *always* meet a doggie...

Co Sligo: This view is from a little road to the north of Yeats's beloved Ben Bulben

Roads among the hills

A little road through the Templederry Hills, Co Tipperary

SINCE prehistoric times little roads have curved among Irish hills and mountains, seeking usually the easiest possible route. Or sometimes folks were seeking the safest route, since danger might lurk in the forested lowlands.

Some roads were pilgrim routes, leading to sacred places; others were simply the only way to go, avoiding lakes, rivers or high mountains.

A road among the Connemara mountains

Silvermines: The road to Keeper Hill

Roads among the hills

Co Louth: Carlingford Mountain (Slieve Foye) seen from Cloghogue, Newry

In the Slieve Bernagh hills

Near Broadford, Co Clare

Glen of Imaal, Co Wicklow

Some of the loveliest panoramas in Ireland can best be seen from a tiny road that winds between hills to suddenly reveal Carlingford Loch, or climbs to the top of Tountinna, from which you can see five counties. Or winds across the Featherbed in the Dublin hills, to open out to the Glencree valley, with its little German war cemetery and that vista of the Sugar Loaf rearing up at the end of the valley.

Not all hill roads take kindly to cars: many have grass up the middle; some simply have no place for cars to pass one another without an agony of reversing. Or you might meet a tractor, pulling some monstrous apparatus that prevents *it* from reversing. Believe me, I've experienced all of it.

So better take a bicycle, or just hike it. Suggestion: whenever you see a hill road that looks interesting, just park the car and get out and walk. Even a short distance can reveal things you never imagined. ∎

Galbally, Co Limerick: Road to the Galtees

The Gap Road in Co Clare

Wind farm in the Silvermines, Co Tipperary

Shaft of sunlight by Loch Derg, seen from Tountinna hill road

*Remember,
you'll always
meet a doggie...*

Lichen-encrusted medieval church and gravestones in east Clare

Textures by the little roads

Near Carna, Co Galway

A ploughed field in Co Kilkenny

PSYCHOLOGIST Carl Jung tells us that (apart from intuition) absolutely all our information comes through the five senses—sight, hearing, touch, taste and smell. But one of the most magical things is that sight and touch are so interlocked that with our eyes alone we can feel the texture of things. I call it touching with the eye.

Now as you travel the little roads you soon become aware of the wonderful textures all around you. You can almost feel them with the eye, without the >>

Textures by the little roads

Roadside in Connemara

Carna, Co Galway

need to touch—the rough edge of lichen; the metallic smoothness of earth after the ploughshare; the delicate surface of new beech leaves.

Lichen can work magic with even the dullest stone. It can bring stunning yellow to a dry-stone wall in Connemara, or white to a ruined church in Co Clare, and can make a landscape vibrate with colour. But

the eye can also sense the surface feel of those stone walls or that high cross, and that sense of touch from a distance can be a sheer joy.

Evening sun can be a wonderful source of texture. A distant field that seemed so smooth at noon can become something you could almost caress when the shadows bring up that distant texture.

And faraway hills,

softened by mist and distance, can look smooth and flat—almost transparent.

Just look at the wet sands of Achill and you can already feel the sand between your toes. And the limestone grikes of the Burren tell your eye just how they would feel were you to touch them.

For seeing is touching from a distance. ∎

A beach near Tramore, Co Waterford

Keel, Achill Island

Youghal, Co Cork

Loch Derg: View from Co Clare

A little road through north Co Cork

Limestone pavement in the Burren

Textured doggie...

21

Spring morning at Flagmount, Co Clare

Roadside patterns

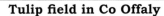

Landscape in north Co Cork

A PATTERN is one of the most satisfying things the eye can discern. Its essence is repetition—mostly a recurring sequence of certain elements, like lines or dots or squares. There are the deliberate ones created by ourselves, such as herringbone tweed, or the drawings of MC Escher.

But it is the patterns in nature that are the most satisfying of all, since we do not create them >>

Monkey-puzzle pattern by Loch Graney

Tulip field in Co Offaly

Roadside patterns

Sometimes a pattern reminds me of Claude Monet's *Water Lilies*

Patterns can be up there..

...or down here

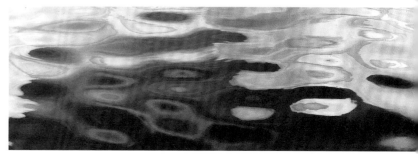

but rather have to discern them—lake water lapping; the widening circles when a stone drops in a pond; ridges on a hillside from long vanished cultivation; the V-formation of migrating geese; the shape of a fern.

Ferns have an especially interesting kind of pattern, since their smaller leaflets are scaled-down approximate copies of the fern itself. And that is repeated on the yet smaller growths that make up the leaflets. This *fractal* pattern, as I think it is called, can be found throughout nature, in clouds, snowflakes, coastlines, trees.

Then there is a phenomenon called the interference or *moiré* pattern. Walk past a row of park railings, with other railings behind it, at right angles. As you walk, the railings play tricks on the eye, appearing thick, then thin, and even seem to dance. Gantries across a motorway play similar tricks: as the car moves towards them the meshes on either side interact, creating what seems like ever bigger meshes.* ∎

* The above passage is excerpted from my book, *The Joy of Looking*

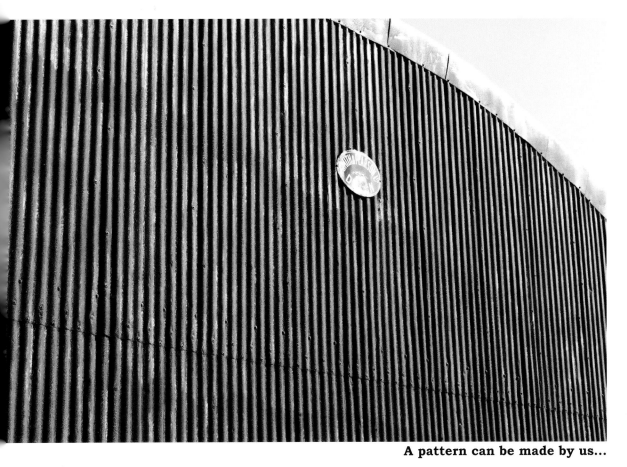

A pattern can be made by us...

Some man-made patterns can be very old...

...and some are quite new

◀ ...or by nature

Ferns show a fractal pattern

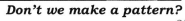

Don't we make a pattern?

No, don't turn me upside down—look at the swans. Loch Graney, Co Clare

Reflections by the roadside

Killaloe Cathedral reflected in the Shannon

Underwater stones yield to sky at Loch Bridget, Co Clare

Loch Ennel, Co Westmeath

ACCORDING to the poet Ovid, Narcissus was such a gorgeous young fellow that, when he went to drink at a forest pool, he fell in love with his own reflection, couldn't reach it and pined away to become eventually a gold-and-white flower. He must have been a bit of an idiot, but our world has a few politicos just like him. Unfortunately they don't seem to do pining.

Reflections may not make us pine away either, but they give astonishing beauty >>

Reflections by the roadside

Honda bike reflects its surroundings

Blue sky dances on Achill beach

to the landscapes along our roads. And the source of most of it is water which, as we know, Ireland has aplenty.

Smooth water is quite simply a plane mirror which gives us a perfect inverted picture of our surroundings. The effect can be lovely—in lakes mirroring swans, in rivers inverting castles and cathedrals.

But a breeze can make it magical, when it softens or elongates those mirror images, or makes them dance to the rhythm of the little waves. As Rupert Brooke put it so beautifully:

There are waters blown by changing winds to laughter
And lit by the rich skies, all day. And after,

Frost, with a gesture, stays the waves that dance
And wandering loveliness. He leaves a white
Unbroken glory, a gathered radiance,
A width, a shining peace, under the night.

All this is part of the magic of reflected light. Eva Gore Booth said something equally lovely:

But the little waves of Breffny have drenched my heart in spray,
And the Little Waves of Breffny go stumbling through my soul.

When I watch such little waves and the reflected light dancing off them, I sometimes wonder, is this the rhythm of the universe—what the Hindus call the Dance of Shiva? ■

Co Wexford: Some of the Seven Castles of Clonmines

A wet road in Co Armagh

Connemara:
Near Carna

By the Royal Canal

Starlings above Loch Derg

Looking up from the road

A fog bow over hill road in Co Tipperary

Vapour trail left by Great-Circle flight

IF you're driving you can't really look at the sky—one good reason to hike or bike the little roads. For you are then free to look up at Ireland's skies. There are all sorts of marvellous things up there that too many of us rarely get to see.

That fog bow, for instance.

I was just walking a hill road when it suddenly appeared. I had never heard of such a thing, so when I got home I typed 'white rainbow' into Google. It explained that water droplets in fog are too tiny to project the rainbow colours. Hence white.

If you practise *pareidolia*—the gift of seeing faces and shapes in random objects—you can have a ball with Irish skies. Just try it—there are cloud faces up there, smiling or glaring down. There are great white birds, and clouds that look like the wings of a dove or an angel. No kidding—take a look at some of the >>

Looking up from the road

A midday sky over Killaloe

Starlings in Donegal

Old man of the sky

What signifies this X in the sky?

pictures here. Our skies are a lot more fun than the boring old blue of the Mediterranean.

Then there are the contrails, or vapour trails. Because Ireland is on the Great Circle route, at any one time there can be lots of planes seven miles up there, creating those beautiful white lines. I have counted up to 17 at any one time.

Those lines start pure and straight, like our innocent lives when young, but then flirt with the winds, lose their true direction, and grow coarse and fat. Some can become a mile wide.

And then of course there are the starlings. Their murmurations can create shapes that look like the plagues of Egypt. No one knows how they do it—one theory is that a single mind takes over, so that the flock becomes temporarily a single living entity of which the starlings become the cells. Like a swarm of bees, perhaps? But we don't really know. ■

A beautiful bird made from vapour trails

The sun is this monster's eye

Atlantic sunset

Spring road in Co Clare

Angel or dove?

I just can't get over them skies...

A united family in Newbridge, Co Kildare

What you might meet along the way

< Highland cattle at Arthurstown, Co Wexford

MUCH of the joy in wandering the little roads of Ireland are the critters you meet along the way. There are always the doggies, of course, but they are just a part of the scenery now.

The cattle are almost as common, forever gazing with curiosity across the gates. If they're not there, just moo and they'll come.

And lots of horses everywhere. Did you ever try imitating a horse's whinny? If you get it right you'll get a whinny right back and the horses will come >>

A herd of wild goats in the Burren, Co Clare

What you might meet along the way

Here are a few of the critters I have encountered while wandering the little roads of Ireland

galloping over to greet you. Their disappointment and contempt, when they realise you're not a horse, is worth experiencing.

Sorry I don't have a squirrel or a badger here— probably because I don't get up early enough. I did meet a badger once in a forest, but I didn't have my camera with me. Sorry. ∎

I'm a sort of sea dog, myself

Light plays on a road in the Silvermines. Did you notice the man's white face?

Let there be light

In the Slieve Aughty Mountains, Co Clare

Light filters through trees in a Sligo woodland

In Ballina, Co Tipperary

Sunlight on a road in Co Galway

EINSTEIN once said, 'All I want to do is study light.' One can see why, for in the end everything comes down to light. And the sight to see the light. Especially for me, the light along the little roads of Ireland.

The late John O'Donohue once wrote of 'those who are physically blind: they have lived all their lives in a moonscape of darkness. They have never seen >>

Let there be light

Komorebi: **When light come through leaves, they glow like a stained-glass window**

Light sculpts the hills at Ogonnelloe, Co Clar

On the road to Castleconnell, Co Limerick

a wave, a stone, a star, a flower, the sky, or the face of another human being.' It is hard for us with vision to imagine how terrible it must be to have no real notion of such things, never having seen them.*

What are the things I would miss, were I to go blind? Well, those things John O'Donohue mentions—waves, stones, stars, flowers, faces. I would miss those beams of light that slant down upon our roads from a sky at evening, and look like a holy picture.

I would miss light filtering through leaves in spring—what the Japanese call *komorebi*. Or the colours in an oil spill on a wet road. Or in a rainbow. Or the slow sparkle on roadstead or harbour as the sun inches westwards. Or a celtic high cross etched against a salmon sky. Or Yeats's long-legged fly upon a stream. Or that golden path to the sun as it sets in the Atlantic. These I have loved. In other words, what I would miss is light. ∎

---

* This passage is excerpted from the author's book, *The Joy of Looking*

Light penetrating grass

Near Cashel, Co Tipperary

Light textures the old red sandstone of the Galtee range

Storm light caresses the Wicklow mountains

Atlantic light in Connemara

How about my rim lighting?

A boreen in County Tipperary

Grass up the middle

Castle Loch, Co Tipperary

This road winds through the Slieve Aughty mountains

TO be considered a boreen, the road or path should not be wide enough for two cars to pass, and have grass growing in the middle.' That's what Wikipedia says, anyhow.

So, if there's grass up the middle, there's not much point in trying to pass another car, or worse still, a tractor. Sometimes there are wide spots for passing, but don't bet on it. As for the grass up the middle, I used to manage to get by with my four-wheel-drive Suzuki Jimny (14 inches above the ground), >>

The road to Slieve Gullion, Co Armagh

Grass up the middle

A little road above Loch Derg

In the hills above Glandore, Co Cork

until I replaced it with a Mazda MX-5 roadster (8 inches above the ground)—dammit I measured them both—so now I have to put the left wheels up on the grass and creep along at 2 km/h. But it certainly cleans the chassis.

So really it makes far more sense to hike or cycle.

But why bother going at all?

Well, simply because these little roads with grass up the middle are the prettiest roads in Ireland, even if they lead you to God-knows-where. ■

Kilbane, Co Clare

Co Sligo: Track to Ben Bulben

In the Slieve Bernagh hills

**Castleconnell
Co Limerick**

Spring landscape at Flagmount, Co Clare

Co Leitrim: A road to God knows where

A back road to Portroe, Co Tipperary

A stand of scots pines on the road to Portroe, Co Tipperary

Trees along the road

Road near Broadford, Co Clare

Trees can sometimes show spooky faces

ONE of the great joys of wandering the little roads are the trees you encounter by the roadside. Trees have been part of the country's psyche since the time of the Druids. It had long been thought that trees harboured spirits, but one thing we now know is that they can communicate with each other, through their roots and through the underground fungi that >>

47

Trees along the road

Poor windswept trees along Atlantic coast roads

link those roots with one another.

Roadside trees have their own special beauty in winter—there are no leaves to hide their dendritic outline, and a tree silhouetted against a sunset, with the trunk bursting into branches and then into smaller ones, all the way to twigs, shows a shape that is incomparable.

It's in all of nature, from the shape of a river with its tributaries fed by tiny streams, to the arteries and veins in our body.

And also our nervous system.

Our Celtic ancestors saw many different trees as sacred—the roots going down to the underworld, and the branches reaching to heaven.

Q. We can tell whether a tree is oak, ash, beech or whatever, by looking at its leaves. But how can we do it in winter, when there are no leaves?

A. It's simple. Don't bother with the tree's shape—just look at the dead leaves under the tree. ∎

Utility poles frequently morph into trees. Culprit is mostly ivy

They still hang rags on sacred trees

◄ ▲ **Roadside trees often have to declare war on roadside walls. The trees mostly win**

I used to be a tree myself...

Road to Bridgetown in Co Clare

Tunnel vision

A tree tunnel in North Cork

THERE are world-famous tree tunnels in many parts of the world, like the Sakura Tunnel in Japan, the Tunnel of Love in the Ukraine, and the Cypress Tunnel in California.

Most were created many years ago by master gardeners and are jealously tended today.

Ireland has dozens of tree tunnels, but hardly any were deliberately created. Trees simply invaded the roadsides, eventually creating a canopy overhead, >>

Quarry Lane, Ballina, Co Tipperary

A tunnel in the hills above Loch Derg

Tunnel vision

Autumn road near Castleconnell, Co Limerick

Near Sixmilebridge, Co Clare

Castle Loch, Co Tipperary

and nobody seemed to mind. About the only tending they ever get is cutting back the edges to stop them from scratching cars.

While many of the world-famous tunnels meet overhead to create a formal space like a gothic cathedral (and probably inspired such cathedrals), Irish tunnels usually form little circles or ovals, like the ones shown here.

It can be a delightful experience to be driving through the countryside and suddenly to plunge into one of these tunnels, with light filtering through the canopy above.

If it's safe to stop the car, do so, and savour the beauty of it. But better still, get yourself a convertible—then you can look up in comfort. Or hike. ■

Road to the Flaggy Shore, Co Clare

A back road to Portroe, Co Tipperary

Powerscourt, Co Wicklow

Evening shadows in Co Galway

Heading for Loop Head

I got tunnel vision...

53

Forest road above Silvermines, Co Tipperary

Forest roads & tracks

Track through the woods in Killarney's National Park

ENTERING a forest track, especially in spring or high summer, can be one of life's most joyful experiences. The birdsong falters for an instant and then resumes with greater vigour. The wind sighs through the foliage, and things rustle in the undergrowth. There is a sense of being watched. Pencils of light slant between the tree trunks leaving pools of brightness on the forest floor.

It is such a joy to wade through a carpet of bluebells that fade into the distance under the trees. Or >>

Forest hillside at Cappoquin, Co Waterford

Woodland drive near Tullamore, Co Offaly

Forests roads and tracks

Silvermines forest road

▲ **Co Clare: This woodland notice speaks for itself** ▶

Rain forest in Co Galway

A little woodland bridge at Garrykennedy, Co Tipperary

to push through a mini forest of ferns between the tree trunks. Or to crunch across a carpet of golden leaves in autumn.

Or to gaze upon branches on the edge of a clearing after a windless snowfall, where every twig seems in blossom from its tiny burden of snow—'midwinter spring' as T.S. Eliot called it.

Or to look at the multicoloured mushrooms and fungi clinging to the tree trunks or covering the forest floor, and remembering that, without the help of those mushrooms, and the hundreds beneath the ground, no tree could grow or thrive.

Or climbing across roots that writhe out of the ground like the sinews of a giant, and realizing they are precisely that—sinews of a giant oak.

A forest offers all of this to those who enter it. But it does more. As Robert Louis Stevenson says: 'It is not so much for its beauty that the forest makes a claim upon men's hearts, as for that subtle something, that quality of air, that emanation from old trees, that so wonderfully changes and renews a weary spirit.'

Benedictine monk Seán Ó Duinn says something similar: 'One feels this strange power especially in woods where the trees seem to wait in suspense and harbour a hidden power.' *■

---

* Excerpted from author's *The Joy of Looking*

Co Limerick: Track through the Clare Glens

The Sugar Loaf seen from Co Wicklow forest

Trees in a forest are like
soldiers, standing up
straight and permitted
hardly any branches ▾ ▸

Tuamgraney Community Native Woodland

This four acre native woodland project is being developed to conserve, enhance, and raise awareness of native biodiversity.

The woodland will act as an outdoor classroom for local schools, who will monitor and study the changes in ecology and biodiversity, as they occur through the seasons.

Invasive non native trees and shrubs have been removed to allow light to penetrate the woodland – this encourages the natural native trees and plants to thrive and in time become a diverse fully functioning native woodland model.

Native deciduous woodlands support a greater variety of species than any other landbased habitat.

Coillearnach [

Tá an tionscadail c
fhorbairt chun bith
a fheabhsú agus fe

Beidh an choill s
áitiúla, agus déanf
na hathruithe éice
tharlaíonn siad le

Tógadh amach c
agus ionracha chu
an choillearnach–:
bhisiú, agus eisea
a bheith ann le bi

57

After rain at Boulavogue, Co Wexford

Roads after rain

A wet little road in South Armagh

After rain in Connemara

Splashes on a Galway road

WHEN I lived in China I used to tell people that the Irish all had webbed feet because of all the rain. When one young lassie asked to see my feet I explained that our religion didn't allow us to show them.

Which was fine until we went swimming together. I had forgotten the lies I had told until, sitting by the edge of the pool with our legs dangling, I heard a contemptuous *Huh* and saw the wee girl glaring at my >>

Roads after rain

A wet little road in south Galway

Hill road near Tountinna, looking towards Limerick

In the hills above Templemore, Co Tipperary

Road near Sixmilebridge, Co Clare

perfectly normal feet.

Maybe we should have webbed feet, given the amount of rain that falls. Or used to, for it seems to have eased off a lot, perhaps due to global warming. We have lately had some really dry summers.

The real nuisance is the unpredictability of the weather. Even forecasters get it wrong. The 12th-century writer Geraldus Cambrensis (aka Gerald of Wales)—no friend of Ireland—was so fed up with the rain here that he christened Ireland 'Jehovah's piss-pot'. But at least the rain keeps Ireland green, meriting a much nicer name, 'The Emerald Isle'—the Germans call it *der grüne Insel*.

Actually it's mostly light showers anyhow and, when the clouds blow away and the sun comes out, the little wet roads sparkle in the sunlight and can become beautiful white ribbons across the landscape. Roads after rain can be surprisingly lovely.

There are times, of course, when the rain is not just a shower but a storm. That's a different matter altogether, as we will see in the next chapter. ■

Above Moneygall, Co Offaly

Clifden, Co Galway: Pot of gold right there

In the Slieve Aughty mountains

I'm not gonna get wet...

Co Tipperary: Storm lashes Tountinna—the 'Fire Mountain' sacred to the Druids

Storm over the road

THE Night of the Big Wind *(Oíche na Gaoithe Móire)* is part of Irish lore. It happened on 6 January 1839, and has never been forgotten. It destroyed houses all over the country, wrecked ships in the harbour, flooded roads, overflowed rivers and killed hundreds. It has been described as Ireland's worst storm in three centuries.

The reason it's so long remembered is that it's so rare a phenomenon. Or rather, was. Global warming is starting to change things. Thank God we still don't have the devastation that New Orleans suffered, nor do we have those tornados that torment America's Midwest. However on 6 September >>

Dark storm clouds over Achill Island

Winter coast at Doolin

An angry Atlantic off Connemara

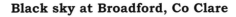

Black sky at Broadford, Co Clare

Storm brewing in Co Galway

63

Storm over the road

Storm gathers over Silvemines cemetery

After the storm on a little road near Broadford, Co Clare

Braving Atlantic winds

Angry ocean at Keel, Achill Island

1961 we got the tail end of Hurricane Debbie when it reached Ireland, still dangerous with peaks of 114 mph. It killed 26, wrecked dozens of homes, destroyed 24 per cent of forests in some areas. It turned mountain streams into raging torrents that swept away ancient stone bridges up in the Wicklow mountains and elsewhere.

Many were replaced by hideous concrete things with circular tunnels instead of the graceful old arches.

Will such storms get more frequent? With global warming, very likely. But it won't keep me off the little roads. In a bad storm, however, I'll stay away from roads with trees, as falling trees have taken many a life.

And in winter storms I would avoid mountain tracks. The Kerry mountains can take lives just as Everest can, if not quite as often. Floods caused by winter storms can play old harry with the sandy surface of a mountain track. It's even worse if motocyclists have cut grooves in the track, as floods can turn those grooves into ravines. ∎

Snow storm over the Slieve Bernagh Mountains

Storm and sunlight in Co Tipperary

Darkness at noon, Co Limerick

Curtains of rain over Loch Ramor, Co Cavan

How I deal with storm...

65

Rush hour in east Galway

Traffic on the little roads

Out for a stroll in Co Clare

Party time in Co Roscommon

Oone of the nicest things about Ireland's marvellous new motorways is, not that they get you there faster, but that they have taken the traffic off the little roads. And good riddance.

These roads have now reverted to the peacefulness of years gone by. Well somewhat—for they still have their traffic problems, the principal one being the cows going to be milked. Twice a day they descend from field to >>

Right of way in Fermoy, Co Cork

Traffic jam near Nenagh, Co Tipperary

Traffic on the little roads

So better not take the car

Milkward bound in Co Carlow

road, where they saunter along with incredible dignity, aware of their importance to the community, and of their priority on the road, and regarding an intruding car with the contempt it deserves.

So what do you do when you encounter the critters? You stop, that's what. Don't try to drive through a herd, if you value your coachwork. But if you stop, the cows will edge past you with considerable consideration and delicacy.

As for sheep, good luck when you encounter them. If it's a flock, there'll be a doggie, who probably will get them by you without trouble. But don't hold your breath. ∎

Speed limit in Co Clare

Busy road in Co Leitrim

Traffic at Clonlara, Co Clare

In Killarney
National Park ▶

I ain't movin' for no traffic...

69

Dawn over Warrenpoint, Co Down

The roads at dawn

Dawn light over a bog road in Co Offaly

Tallaght-Kilbride road, Dublin Mountains

'DEATH is not extinguishing the light; it is only putting out the lamp because the dawn has come.'

As I grow older, those words of Rabindranath Tagore come to my mind every time I watch a dawn. Which is not as often as I used to. But when I do go out early on one of the little roads in the hills where I live, what I see can move me greatly.

There is the lightening sky when the sun is still 12 degrees below the horizon (what sailors call the nautical dawn); then the shadows >>

Early morning in Co Longford

Morning dew collects on spiders' webs

The roads at dawn

Morning fog creates this white sea at Grange, Killaloe, Co Clare

Dawn sky in Co Longford

Dew-drenched grass at dawn

Long shadows above the Shannon in Co Limerick

that creep across the fields as the sun comes up.

Then the way a green field seems to glow almost yellow-green as the light penetrates each blade of grass before it reaches you; and the sparkle of the dew on the grass. The painter Constable was the first to depict such magic, and people mocked his sparkle as 'Constable's snow.' They don't mock now.

Dawn mist for me is the essence of the morning magic. It can fill a valley like a white sea; it can soften winter trees and make hillsides recede into ghostly distance. As Paul Laurence Dunbar once wrote—

An angel, robed in spotless white,
Bent down and kissed the sleeping Night.
Night woke to blush; the sprite was gone.
Men saw the blush and called it Dawn. ■

The magic of early mist near Dromineer, Co Tipperary

Morning on the Shannon at Castleconnell

Early walkers enjoy the golden light of morning

Dew clings to spider webs

Co Cork: The rising sun casts long shadows

Barking to greet the dawn...

An evening road in east Limerick

The little roads at evening

Atlantic sundown in Connemara

Shannon airport seen from Cratloe hill road

Cloughogue, Newry, Co Down

Co Leitrim sunset

Co Westmeath: Lake Derravaragh at evening

'WE are all naturally seekers of wonders. We travel far to see the majesty of the hoary mountains, great waterfalls, and galleries of art. And yet the world's wonder is all around us; the wonder of setting suns, and evening stars...'

These words of Albert Pike sum up for me what evening means. It means a dark blue sky descending into orange towards the horizon, so that it is impossible to see exactly >>

The little roads at evening

Evening comes to the Silvermines

The road to Portroe, Co Tipperary

Dying sun reflections in River Shannon at Ballina

where one colour yields to the other.

It means the salmon pink of those Atlantic clouds when the sun is low; or the sun perched on that hilltop and seeming to spin before it slides out of sight.

Or the rare Green Flash as it disappears, which I have seen only once in my life.

It means mountains receding into distant mauve; fields revealing their texture in the slanting light; the water that 'mirrors a still sky', which rejoiced Yeats among the wild swans of Coole. All of this for me is the Celtic Twilight, which our little roads reveal so splendidly, but little of which can be seen in city streets.

We all know the dawn chorus (if we get up early enough), but there's also an evening chorus which is equally lovely. And which momentarily seems to hush as the last spark of the sun is quenched.

And at evening I can watch the shadows of the hedgerows extend across the sward like long fingers. The sight of those shadows always recalls for me the words of Cardinal Newman:

O Lord
support us all day long until the shadows lengthen
and the evening comes

and the fever of life is over
And our work is done. ■

Airbus and Atlantic sunset together made this vapour trail

A sunset sky over Roundstone, Co Galway

Winter evening near Blessington

Evening sun creates long shadows beside this farmhouse in Co Clare

And I too cast a long shadow ▶

Orion over Killaloe, Co Clare

Night upon the roads

Duncannon, Co Wexford

Carna, Co Galway

Mount Melleray Abbey, Co Waterford

JEWISH festivals begin at the start of the night before—when the first three stars are visible. For night is a wonderful time to prepare and contemplate. But it is so difficult in a city or town. And that is when the little roads come into their own.

It is only on a dark road, far away from ambient city lights, that we encounter the universe, if the sky be cloudless; or can experience the haunting light of the moon; or sometimes meet the most total darkness >>

Night upon the roads

A lonely walk by the Shannon

Night falls on Millstreet, Co Cork

Co Down: Mountain road gives this view of Newry canal

we may ever encounter.

A sky filled with stars is quite literally our only glimpse of the universe. Just to lean back and gaze can be a spiritual experience, of the immensity out there and of our own minuteness.

It is here too that we encounter silence—something we rarely experience, but desperately need. As Mother Theresa said, 'See how nature—trees, flowers, grass—grows in silence; see the stars, the moon and the sun, how they move in silence... We need silence to be able to touch souls.'

A moonless, starless night can be a special experience. The total darkness of a country road can be daunting to us who are never far from city lights, but it can have an extraordinary effect if we let it engulf us. Perspectives can alter; things that bothered us can seem trivial; enmities and resentments fade. Hillary Clinton puts it beautifully: 'One feels that resurrection of hope in the midst of despair and apathy.'

One caution, however: Never walk a country road without a high-viz reflector jacket. All the spiritual experiences in the world will not save you from a car driver who cannot see you. ■

Winter nightfall in north Tipperary

Night by the Lakes of Killarney

Valentia, Co Kerry

Waterford celebrates

They won't let me out at night...

Gateway into a field on Inchydoney Island, Co Cork

Gateways along the road

Ballina, Co Tipperary

Gateway to Clare Abbey, Ennis, Co Clare

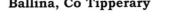

WALLS have been basic to human existence since Adam was a boy. I mean, there would surely have been one around the Garden of Eden, to prevent him and Eve from getting back in.

Some walls are to keep folks out, like the Great Wall of China or the Gates of Heaven; others to keep people in, like the Berlin Wall. And others are just to show who owns what. But since we're not supposed >>

Gateways along the road

Co Offaly: Slieve Bloom mountains

Near Clonakilty, Co Cork

In the Silvermines, Co Tipperary

to climb walls, they all need gateways.

The little roads of Ireland have their walls too—the dry-stone walls of Connemara, or their equivalent as hedges, ditches or fences elsewhere. All have the same functions—to keep livestock in, and to keep us out (so we don't trample crops or get killed by a bull). And they also show who owns what field. Naturally there are gateways, to let cattle in and out, or let a tractor in. Many gateways, however, have what sociologists term a latent function—one unintended— they are windows onto the landscape. Irish farmers have a nasty tendency to let hedges grow high, so it's a relief to reach a gateway and get a glimpse into a lovely panorama of fields and hillside.

Gateways may indeed be windows into beauty, but the gates themselves are for respecting. When I was four years old my mother took my six-year-old brother and myself into a hilly field for a picnic. We were just inside the field when suddenly over the crest of the hill thundered a charging herd of cattle.

Ma simply threw my brother and me over the gate and vaulted it herself—she was very athletic. Ever since then I have respected gates and been wary of entering fields, however lovely. Especially if I see a notice saying *Beware of the Bull*. But I will always pause to peep through a gateway. ∎

Gate guardian, Ruan, Co Clare

Co Roscommon: Road to Loch Arrow

Dingle, Co Kerry

Open gate near Portroe, Co Tipperary

Gateway overlooking Loch Derg

Keeps us in, and you out...

Spring comes to the Shannon at Killaloe

Spring comes to the roads

THE concept of *Ukiyo*—The Floating World—is deeply rooted in the mind of every Japanese. It comes from Buddhism, the kernel of which is that everything is transient, nothing lasts: all our joys, hopes, beauty, love and even life itself are floating away from us and will soon be gone.

For the Japanese, the symbol of all this is the cherry blossom. Its beauty can take our breath away, but a puff of wind can take the blossom away. So, being an eminently practical people, the Japanese take off in droves every spring to view the cherry blossoms >>

Spring near Ballymena, Co Antrim

Bloody Crane's Bill in the grikes of the Burren

They call it gorse, furze or whins

Spring comes to the roads

Roadside shrine at Tuamgraney, Co Clare

Daffodils in my garden above the Shannon

—a bit like the way certain of our fishing fraternity call in sick when the mayfly rises. Perhaps there is something to be learnt from the Japanese. And not just about cherry blossoms, but about nature itself, especially in springtime along our little roads.

For years I used to look forward to the first primrose by the roadside, but when it came I was too busy to give it more than a cursory glance. Then, like the cherry blossom, it was gone. Then the daffodils came and they went too. Then would come the year's most magical 10 days, during which green slowly seeps along the hedgerows—that early green of a freshness and brilliance that has no equal in nature.

I'd be sort of aware of it through the car windows as I'd go about my urgent and important business— whatever it happened to be at the time—and I would tell myself that yes I must take a bit of time off to climb out onto the road and have a look. When I could find time, that is.

Mostly I didn't. And usually by the time I did— if I did—the green had darkened and the blossoms were on the ground.

All that is a long time ago. Nowadays I make time for spring. And all that urgent business mostly turns out to be not that urgent at all. Whereas spring *is* urgent, for it simply won't wait. And besides, how many more springs do I have?* ■

* Excerpted from the author's book, *The Joy of Looking*

Co Meath: by Loch Sheelan's side, this little mayfly landed on my windscreen

Hill road near Birdhill, Co Tipperary

Mayflies on my car boot, all facing north

Road by The Flaggy Shore, Co Clare

The arrival of summer

Co Galway: When summer comes to the woodlands

I LATELY saw a photo in some magazine of a Spanish beach in high summer and I shivered at the horror of it. Hundreds of half-naked bodies packed tightly, sweating and roasting in the sun, like sausages on a pan. Beside it was another photo of hundreds of people sitting and standing and lying in a crowded airport waiting for hours for a plane that doesn't come.

A roadside church near Cloughjordan, Co Tipperary

A summer roadside in Co Leitrim

The arrival of summer

As kids we called them 'brown billies'—tortoise-shells gorging at a summer picnic

Co Galway: White roadsides in early summer

So if I travel or holiday abroad I do it in any other season. Summer to me is for exploring the little roads of Ireland. I know no greater joy.

It is the season when Ireland erupts into colour—roadsides blazing red with montbretia; then the dazzling yellow of a rapeseed field; fuschia tumbling over walls and alive with bees.

Have you ever noticed how a fuschia bloom looks like a little ballerina? Take a look at the photo on the previous page—there's a tiny head, a little red body, a flaring skirt and dangling legs.

Then of course there's the buddleia—the butterfly tree—in lilac, white, blue or dark purple, which is spreading with such rapidity in recent years. As BBC weather forecaster Peter Gibbs says, 'Buddleia is an opportunist that's always ready to capitalise on any slight advantage.'

The loneliness is one lovely thing about our roads. You hardly meet a soul and when you do there is a friendly greeting and a sharing of summer joy.

And finally there's the pub at the end of the road. GK Chesterton got it right when he wrote, 'Let a man walk 10 miles steadily on a hot summer's day... and he will soon discover why beer was invented.' ■

Rapeseed blossom in Co Wicklow

Summer road near Ballinahinch, Co Tipperary

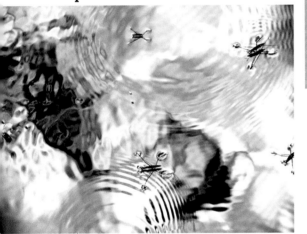

Walking on water on the Scariff river

Thrift blossoms by cliff road in West Cork

Not quite Van Gogh: Crows on a field in Co Clare

The little roads in autumn

Cross-border road from the Flagstaff to Omeath, Co Louth

VAN GOGH's last painting before he killed himself was of crows in a wheat field. I got something slightly like that last autumn (opposite page), but I'm planning on staying alive.

I can however understand how Van Gogh might have felt, for autumn can be sad.

But also glad.

There's the sadness of letting go—we must let go of summer >>

The little roads in autumn

Autumn in north Clare

as the trees let go of their leaves. But there is gladness too—in the harvest bounty of *Samhain*, in the apples in our orchards, in the blackberries lining our roadsides on which I gorged as a boy, and sometimes still do.

But the most gladdening thing of all are the leaves of autumn. As Albert Camus said, 'Autumn is a second spring, where every leaf is a flower.' Few things are lovelier than those leaves, or sadder than seeing them flutter to the ground.

One truly lovely thing on an autumn road is the dance of the leaves. A sudden little breeze can make dead leaves come alive, to rise up and pirouette in the middle of the road for a few magic moments before collapsing from exhaustion.

I watch and wait for that dance every autumn.

I think autumn has a profound lesson for all of us as we grow inexorably older. It's this—as the years pass there are things we simply have to let go. Perhaps letting go of our children as they grow up and leave, or letting go of our nimbleness as the body ages. We can surely learn from the trees who let their leaves go with such grace and beauty. ■

Harvest time in south Galway

Fall comes to Co Derry

Gettin' cold out here...

The Reeks under snow in Kerry

The grip of winter

The Gap Road in east Clare

The road to Portroe, Co Tipperary

THE Venerable Bede wrote the following in 731 AD: 'Ireland is broader than Britain, is healthier and has a much milder climate, so that snow rarely lasts for more than three days. Hay is never cut in summer for winter use nor are stables built for their beasts.

'No reptile is found there nor could a serpent survive; for although serpents have often >>

Snow storm in Glenties, Co Donegal

The grip of winter

Near Piper's Inn, Slieve Bernagh hills, Co Clare

Most years deep snow and flooding are just occasional. But climate change is worrying

been brought from Britain, as soon as the ship approaches land they are affected by the scent of the air and quickly perish.'

I don't believe the half of it, but I would accept what Bede said about snow—it rarely lasts more than a few days. But when it does come, especially on a windless night, the roadside hedgerows blossom pure white, with every little twig bearing its tiny line of snow.

TS Eliot memorably called it 'midwinter spring'.

Snow may be lovely along the little roads for a while after it falls, but it becomes horrible when the thaw comes. I sometimes think snow is like a bad marriage—it starts white and pure and fresh and lovely, full of hope and promise. But all too soon it turns nasty, slippery and treacherous, leaving us longing for it all just to end.

Snow is at its best when it keeps to the mountains,

making a stunning backdrop to our roads. And that is where it belongs.

Wet winter roads under a drizzling dreary sky are Ireland's least attractive offering. But the country's daft weather means that it can suddenly turn to sunshine. And then we can watch scudding clouds, V-formations of hurrying geese, and those glorious sunsets which come so conveniently early in winter.■

Winter landscape: Keeper Hill and the Silvermines

Shannon in flood at O'Brien's Bridge, Co Clare

Co Westmeath: Flooding near Athlone

▲ A trespassing fox left these imprints

Co Tipperary: Slate quarries

Rudolph at the Galway Clinic

Wouldn't dream of going out in this weather ▸

Preserved at the old Clifden railway station, this 1925 tourist poster helped make Paul Henry famous worldwide

In search of Paul Henry

A road into the Twelve Bens

Croagh Patrick: Ireland's pilgrim mountain

IN 1925 the London Midland and Scottish Railway (LMS) published a tourist poster using a painting by Belfast-born artist Paul Henry. It created a sensation, creating worldwide awareness of the haunting beauty of the West of Ireland.

As *The Irish Times* wrote at the time, 'If thousands of people in Great Britain >>

Connemara: Evening light near Carna

In search of Paul Henry

and America have been led this summer to think over the claims of Ireland as holiday ground, it is largely through the lure of Mr Paul Henry's glowing landscape of a Connemara scene.'

Indeed Paul Henry's towering clouds, purple mountains and tiny white cottages have defined western Irish landscape for almost a century.

But is that landscape still there? I set out with my camera to find out. Obviously I don't have the eye of Paul Henry, but I did discover scenes not all that different from what he saw in Achill and Connemara and Kerry.

The houses have changed, thank God, from the miserable cabins of his time, but the neat new bungalows are still tiny white objects clinging to the foot of mountains as if seeking shelter and protection. The great Atlantic clouds still soar high above the Twelve Bens and Achill's Slievemore, and the mountains still recede at evening into that distant purple. The Paul Henry country is still unique. ■

Connemara seen from the Atlantic seaboard

A little road into the mountains near Recess

Atlantic clouds soar above the Twelve Bens

Beyond Oughterard, a tiny house seems to seek shelter from the mountain

An Achill Island vista

In search of Paul Henry

Killarney: Evening over Loch Leane

Slievemore, Achill Island

Beyond Maam Cross

Road to the Twelve Bens

Donegal's Blue Stack mountains

Near Carraroe, Co Galway

A gathering storm over Connemara

Connemara ponies in Connemara

Love by the roadside

L OOK carefully when you
wander the little roads,
and you will see many
beautiful signs of love between
animals—even between such
different species as dog and
cat. On these pages I show
a few of the lovers I have
encountered.

But dare we call it love? We
are warned about attributing
human emotions to animals,
since they can't tell us exactly
how they feel.

Love by the roadside

There has been some progress on this question. Gregory Berns, a neuroscientist at America's Emory University, used fMRI imaging on dogs' brains, and found indications of empathy and attachment.

Experiments by Harry Harlow, research psychologist at the University of Wisconsin-Madison, have been accepted by some scientists as demonstrating that animals can love and can matter to one another.

Stephen Marc Breedlove, of Michigan State University, says we have seen 'a change in the zeitgeist... People are open to the possibility that animals have emotions.'

One last thing. The hormone *oxytocin*, which is crucial for us in social bonding and love, has also been found in animals.

All the above is just stuff I have read, as I have not the slightest expertise in the subject. But one thing I do know for certain—I have seen for myself what looks very like love in some of God's creatures, and I have photographed it. ■

Could these kissing ferns be in love?

◄ **Maternal love and—uh—other kinds** ▲

But always a doggie or two...

A wayside memorial at the summit of the hill road to Kilbane, Co Clare

Sadness by the roadside

Result of emigration?

KILNABARNAN
Children's
Burial Ground

ERECTED TO THE MEMORY
OF THOSE BURIED HERE

Refurbished and Blessed

2003

WHEREVER you go along the little roads you are sure to come across strange little fields bumpy with mounds and stones. These are *kileens*, burial grounds for unbaptized infants who would never see the face of God—so people believed—and so could not be buried in consecrated ground. Now at least many have a commemorative plaque honoring these grievously wronged little ones.

There is a custom in rural Ireland to put a cross or memorial stone on the spot where someone died or was killed in an accident. People leave flowers at these tiny >>

Swan mourned by its mate at Castle Loch, Co Tipperary. Swans mate for life

"A Stolen Ringbuoy
A Stolen Life"

www.iws.ie

Burial ground for unbaptised infants at Kilnabarnan, Co Clare

Sadness by the roadside

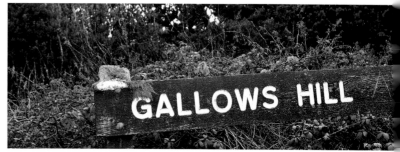

GALLOWS HILL

Where they used hang folks near Bunratty, Co Clare

'*A mon Papa*' : Bantry memorial to the Betelguese dead

Grief oozes from these workhouse walls, at Bawnboy, Co Cavan

shrines for years afterwards.

While I get such joy from wandering the little roads of Ireland, spots like these make for momentary sadness, and I sometimes say a prayer for whoever died here.

What else on the roadside makes me sad? A dead animal, ignored by traffic. A child's doll lying on the road. Decay anywhere—a roofless, windowless house around which children must once have played. A wrecked car lying in the ditch waiting to be removed. Did anyone die in it? Refuse dumped in a ditch, revealing that some people can still be incredibly selfish.

Places like Gallows Hill, reminding us of the incredible savagery of times past. Cemeteries too make me sad, especially those with leaning abandoned tombstones.

And shuttered pubs along the way—there are many of these, due to the new drink-driving laws. But I think of lonely folks from the hills who have nowhere now to go on a Saturday night.

And then I think of far sadder roads in other lands today, echoing to the tramp of refugees or famine victims, and I thank God that our roads are so tranquil.

They weren't always, however, as the next chapter remembers. ■

Rust in Carlingford Loch

Pray for whoever Billy is...

114

Cloghogue, Newry: I used to walk this little road as a boy. Now no one can

The sadness of
abandoned things ▾ ▴ ▸

Where they shot Michael Collins in 1922

I don't DO sad...!

115

The Céide Fields in Co Mayo, the oldest-known field system in the world, goes back 5,500 years

Pre-history & myth

Entrance to stone circle at Loch Gur, Co Limerick

The Brown Bull of Cooley

WHATEVER road you take, you are in touch with Ireland's pre-history, recalled by stone circles and dolmens throughout the land, by places associated with the ancient myths, and sculptures recalling them.

For example, the Brown Bull of Cooley, a bronze replica of which stands by the Carlingford-Dundalk road on the Cooley Peninsula. It recalls the Cattle Raid of Cooley, when Queen Maeve of Connacht tried to capture King Conor of Ulster's celebrated brown bull. It led to all >>

Craggaunowen replica Bronze-Age village

117

Pre-history & myth

One of the Children of Lir at sundown on Lake Derravaragh, Co Westmeath

sorts of shenanigans involving Cúchulainn, the superhero of the era.

Go to Lake Derravaragh in Co Westmeath, where a wicked stepmother turned the King's kiddies into four swans. They're still there, by the way. I photographed them, so that proves it. (Incidentally, why are poor old stepmothers always considered wicked?)

Myths aside, real people lived in Ireland during the Paleolithic, Mesolithic, Neolithic, Bronze and Iron ages and they have left their traces along many of our little roads. There are more than 1,200 monuments from the Neolithic period (4000 to 2500 BC), the most impressive being the passage tomb at Newgrange, Co Louth, dating from about 3200 BC (centuries before the Giza Pyramids).

There are also court cairns, wedge tombs and dolmens (portal tombs), best-known of which is at Poulnabrone, in the Burren.

Later came the fascinating stone circles, dating from 2500 to 1000 BC, the largest and most impressive being at Grange, near Loch Gur in Co Limerick (two pictures of it here).

Many of these monuments are easily accessible from our roads. ■

365-million-year-old tetrapod footprints at Valentia, Co Kerry

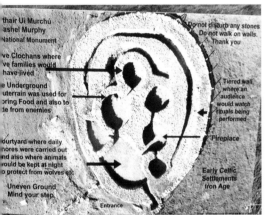

thair Uí Murchú
ashel Murphy
National Monument

ve Clochans where
ve families would
have lived

e Underground
uterrain was used for
oring Food and also to
de from enemies

ourtyard where daily
nores were carried out
nd also where animals
vould be kept at night
o protect from wolves etc

Uneven Ground
Mind your step

Entrance

Do not disturb any stones
Do not walk on walls.
Thank you

Tiered wall
where an
audience
would watch
rituals being
performed

Fireplace

Early Celtic
Settlements
Iron Age

◄ Cashel Murphy, Iron-Age settlement on Dingle Peninsula

Stone circle in the Bernish, Co Armagh

Stone circle in north Co Clare

Your author squares up to phallic symbol near Rearcross, Co Tipperary

Ireland's largest stone circle at Loch Gur, Co Limerick

Dolmen in west Co Cork

Nothing new under the sun...

Quin Friary, Co Clare: Cromwell murdered the Franciscan friars in 1650, but there was still a friar here, John Hogan, until 1820

Roads into history

Co Kerry: Carrigafoyle Castle defenders massacred in 1580

Were these the sculptor's fellow monks?

Co Antrim: Memorial plaque in Larne

Grace O'Malley's castle overlooks Achill Sound

THE stark ruin of Carrigafoyle Castle stands at the Co Kerry end of the Shannon estuary. In 1580 after a ferocious siege, the survivors of 50 Irish rebels and 16 Spanish soldiers, and also one woman, were taken back to the English camp and hanged from trees.

Some time ago, as I was taking photos of the castle, I heard the voices of happy children from a family picnicking nearby, and I at once remembered the words of hunger >>

Roads into history

Plaque at Moneygall, Co Tipperary, commemorating the 2011 visit of US President Barack Obama

Rosmuc, Co Galway: Cottage of Pádraic Pearse, 1916 leader, is now a shrine and a museum

striker Bobby Sands: 'Our revenge will be the laughter of our children.'

Chesterton got it wrong when he said that all our wars were merry and all our songs were sad. There was little merriment in the centuries from the Viking raids to the Norman invasion, to the Famine, to 1916, to the civil war that followed, or to the Northern Ireland troubles.

It's all over now, *we hope*, and our roads do echo the laughter of our children. But those same roads, wherever we go, put right in our faces the reminders of our grim history. Ruined castles, skeletal suppressed monasteries, sites of battles, places of execution, memorials to martyrs—there is no escaping them as we wander the roads.

Yet these are perhaps the most fascinating aspects of our roads. The travail is over, thank God, and we can ponder with a sense of gratitude that it is indeed over.

And we can also rejoice in the positive things of our history, such as Sarsfield's brilliant ride to blow up King William's ammunition train during the 1690 siege of Limerick.

There are road signs all through Clare and Tipperary that enable us to follow the precise route he took, and it's a wonderful trip to take.

Our roads are steeped in history and we can see it in the very stones. There is simply no escaping it, for which I am profoundly grateful. ■

Duncannon Fort, Co Wexford

SARSFIELD'S RIDE
1690

Both sides are remembered at this memorial of the battle of Keimaneigh, in Co Cork

TO COMMEMORATE THOSE WHO DIED
AT AND AFTER THE
BATTLE OF KEIMANEIGH
JANUARY 1822.
MICHAEL CASEY. BARRY O'LEARY.
AULIFFE LYNCH. EDWARD RING.
(LOCAL WHITEBOYS)
JOHN SMITH (CROWN FORCES).
MAY THEY REST IN PEACE.

Shanid Castle, Co Limerick, burnt 1641, was early stronghold of the Knights of Glin

Motte & bailey at Kerrin, Co Tipperary

Tomb of St Patrick at Downpatrick Cathedral ?

Watching for them Vikings...

On this lovely road in Achill, people wandered starving and dying, in the Great Famine of 1847

Famine roads

This cross, outside Limerick, marks the site of a mass grave of victims of the Great Famine of 1847

IN MEMORY OF
ALL WHO DIED
KNOWN AND UNKNOWN
DURING THE FAMINE.

ERECTED BY THE
BALLINAKILL/DERRYBRIEN
PARISHIONERS.

REST IN PEACE.
2000 A. D.

Memorial at Ballinakill, County Laois

WHEN I have been wandering certain roads, I have sometimes experienced a sense of inexplicable grief. It is only when I realise that these were roads where famine victims must have wandered, that I begin perhaps to understand.

Scientist Rupert Sheldrake's theory of morphic resonance (frowned upon by some scientists) holds that >>

Kinvarra, Co Galway: Road to a famine mass grave

Famine roads

Elphin, Co Leitrim: Famine soup-kitchen bowl. Soup cancelled at height of the Famine

Deserted cottages in north Mayo

Plaque in Sligo tells its own story

terrain and even stones can absorb and 'remember' things that happened in their vicinity. I certainly felt something in Auschwitz, but I have also felt this grief on certain Irish roads.

Perhaps it's nonsense, and it's that I was aware of the history before I felt the sadness. But not quite so: I have felt this grief and only later realised that these had been famine roads. Who will ever know?

But I also still feel anger at what happened all those years ago. When I see the ruined houses along the road, when I realise that people did wander starving and dying where I now walk in peace and comfort, I can feel anger. Especially when I read that Sir Charles Trevelyan notoriously said, 'The judgement of God sent the calamity to teach the Irish a lesson.' He also said famine was an 'effective mechanism for reducing surplus population.' Then I think that similar things are taking place right now in other parts of the world, and I ask myself, am I as indifferent to that as the non-starving were, all those years ago? ■

Mt Charles: Donegal devastated

Famine road in Achill

...and a hardly readable stone like this... 'To the memory of unnamed victims of famine who died during 1845 to 1847, and were buried here. Ar neamh doibh uilig' ▾

Kinvarra, Co Galway: *Instead of this...*

...thousands upon thousands got this...

And this is what was left...

And here is where they lie today...

Some escaped on famine ships like this replica in New Ross. But thousands died and were buried at sea

127

The road north of Mulranny, County Mayo

The serpentine shape

Road near Loch Graney, Co Clare

A laneway in Co Carlow

Road to Slievemore, Achill Island

By Loch Allen, Co Leitrim

HOGARTH's *Line of Beauty* was an insight by the 18th-century English painter, who maintained that the serpentine shape—an undulating curved line—is more pleasing to the eye than a boring old straight line. It is certainly true of Ireland's little roads.

William Hogarth would have loved them. For they are truly serpentine, curving all over the place. Far from being designed for beauty, however, they simply had to get by obstacles >>

The serpentine shape

Seashore in Co Wexford

Narrow Water & Carlingford Loch separate Northern Ireland from the Irish Republic

Hill road in Co Clare

like rocks and hills and bogs. The curving S-shape was the result. In early days mostly the cows decided where to go, and we just followed. The cow roads *(bóthair)* eventually solidified into the little roads we know today.

In his *Analysis of Beauty* (1753), Hogarth says that S-shaped lines suggest liveliness and movement and fun—in other words, life—in contrast to dreary old straight lines, or worse still, crossed lines, which suggest death.

Perhaps this is why we find Ireland's superb new motorways boring. They certainly get you there, and brilliantly, but those straight lines, converging on a vanishing point in the distance, just go on and on with no variety, until you want to fall asleep at the wheel. Which can happen.

But there's no way you could fall asleep on a little country road that winds all over the place. Actually one of the loveliest things about the little roads is the sudden vista or flash of beauty that you can encounter when you come around a bend. The joy of the serpentine shape is what it hides and suddenly reveals.

Hogarth's *Line of Beauty* is also true of many things we encounter on the roads. The neck of a swan; the curve of a cloud; hedges running around hillsides; the meandering of a river. It's what makes the Hidden Ireland so lovely. ■

Near Kinvarra, Co Galway

Serpentine shape can be wall, sky, swan, even cactus

Serpentine foam in north Donegal

Serpentine
‹ *doggie*

A little farm track in east Clare

Little roadside lake near Mweenish, Co Galway. Those are the Twelve Bens on the horizon

Peaceful roads

A mountain road in east Clare

SOME little roads seem to exude peacefulness. It can hardly be the road itself, surely, but perhaps whatever I see from the road—like a peaceful little lake in Connemara, or a boat moored at evening on a quiet fisherman's lake, or a silent swan at evening. One can feel such peace especially when walking, and even more when walking alone, but rarely when rushing by in a car with the radio on.

Is there something special about such roads? Or is it something >>

Evening at Loch Cutra, Co Galway

A swan at evening on Lake Derravaragh, Co Westmeath

Peaceful roads

A little road by the sea in north Co Clare

Wicklow: Glencree has Centre for Peace & Reconciliation

we bring to them? I believe it is both.

Beauty and tranquillity seem to be preconditions that allow us to live in the moment—*if we are ready to*. But that can only happen if we come to such a road prepared for a brief while to let go of all our preoccupations of present, past or future, thus allowing us to live in the here and now. Which is where peace is found.

This living in the Now can be difficult to achieve, since, as Buddhist monk Thich Nhat Hanh says, 'Because our minds are elsewhere, we are not walking with our full body and our full consciousness. We see our minds and our bodies as two separate things. While our bodies are walking one way, our consciousness is tugging us in a different direction.'

But if on the road you can get it right, you will arrive in the here and now.

Thich Nhat Hanh again: 'And suddenly you are free—free from all projects, all worries, all expectations. You are fully present, fully alive, and you are touching the earth.'

In other words, you are at peace. ∎

Peaceful sketching in Westport, Co Galway

Diarmuid & Grainne at peace in Kilbaha, Loop Head

A peaceful evening at Loch Derg

We don't just *fly* through clouds...

South Armagh, once more at peace

Templemore, Co Tipperary

Rural road in Co Galway

We come in peace...

135

A bridge at Westport, Co Mayo

Roads over bridges

THE little roads are forever meeting rivers and canals, so Ireland has a multitude of bridges. Many are stone bridges built several centuries ago. Yet most of us never see them since we simply drive over them. We just feel a slight bump and then we are gone. And so is the bridge, for us anyway.

For years I have made a point of stopping the car and going down the path to the river or canal, to get a view of the bridge. There is nearly always a path worn by fishermen. What I see can often evoke both wonder and gratitude.

Swans at evening by O'Brien's Bridge, Co Clare

Brickeen Bridge, Lakes of Killarney

A tiny ancient bridge in Connemara

Roads over bridges

Co Offaly: Bridge across the Grand Canal

Nenagh River crossing, Co Tipperary

Bridge across the Shannon at Killaloe, Co Clare

The wonder at how folks of the 17th or 18th centuries and indeed earlier, without modern technology, could have constructed those elegant arches with their keystones holding all in place. Of course the Romans were doing it thousands of years ago, so their achievements were there to be learnt from.

I also feel gratitude to those anonymous workers who have left us this heritage which we drive across and take for granted. And I feel amazement at the great viaducts of the 19th century, like the Craigmore Viaduct at Bessbrook, Co Down, with its 18 arches. As children we used to be told that during its construction a man died for every arch.

One of the most amazing bridges in Ireland is hardly ever seen. It is the gothic-bridge over the gorge at Poulaphuca in Co Wicklow. It takes some climbing down to get to see it, but worth it. To me it's like a cathedral perched atop the gorge. It was designed by Alexander Nimmo, who also built some of our best-known piers and harbours. Unfortunately I do not have a photo to show you—next edition, perhaps? ∎

Co Waterford: The Durrow Viaduct once carried trains...

...now it's a superb walkway

Bessbrook, Co Down: Craigmore Viaduct has 18 arches

Co Cavan: Bridge over the source of the Shannon

Ancient hump-backed bridge in Connemara

Bridge linking Achill Island with mainland

An overpass across the M7...

carries this road...

which immediately narrows...

to become this...   *and end in a farmyard*

Skyline near Ardnacrusha, Co Clare

Skylines above the road

Skyline in the Slieve Bernagh hills

ONE of the best reasons for hiking rather than driving the little roads is that you can look up from the road since you are not driving. I've already mentioned what you can see in the sky but, before you ever reach the sky, there is the skyline. And Irish skylines can be very lovely indeed.

Part of their beauty is that they are so often silhouettes against the sky. The outline of winter trees, a ruin atop a hill, a dry-stone wall along a hilltop, with the light peeping through the stones.

One of my favourite skylines is the Devil's Bit in Co Tipperary, where >>

The Devil's Bit mountain, Co Tipperary

Windmills against a Co Kerry skyline

Skylines above the road

Hill road in the Slieve Blooms

Sunset skyline near Dungannon

A field near Omagh, Co Tyrone

the skyline shows a mighty gap. Legend has it that the Devil took a bite out of the mountain, broke a tooth in the process, and spat the bite out, which then became the Rock of Cashel.

There's a lot of fuss at the moment about skylines being ruined by those new windmills constructed for renewable energy. Every language has its version of there's-no-accounting-for-tastes, so all I can say here is that I think the windmills are very beautiful. The elegance of the silhouettes, the gracefulness of the slow-moving blades, are a truly lovely addition to our skylines.

People kicked up murder when the Eiffel Tower was built in Paris, but everyone loves it now.

I do believe that our windmills will become cherished when the fuss dies down and the years go by, and will be as important a part of our landscapes as the old windmills are to Holland.

What we need are a few artists to paint them into their landscapes and perhaps then people will change their minds. ■

Dry-stone wall on a Connemara skyline

Wind farm in Co Tipperary

Familiar landmark on the Nenagh-Thurles road

Co Mayo: Pilgrim path leads up Croagh Patrick, Ireland's sacred mountain, said to be climbed by one million pilgrims a year. View from across Clew Bay

Pilgrim paths & sacred places

Co Mayo: Ballintubber Abbey is a famous pilgrim destination

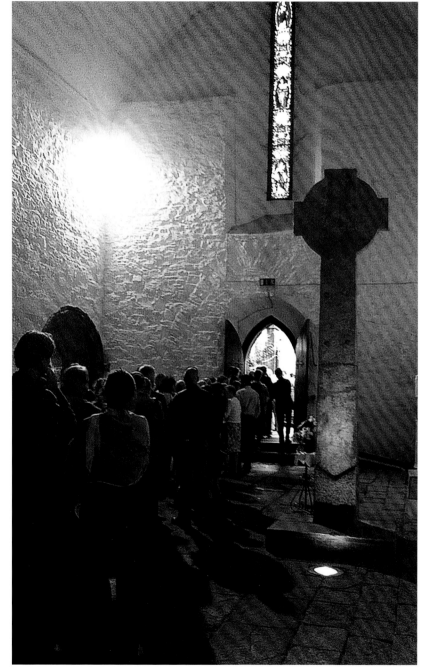

IT all began with the Druids of ancient Ireland. They had their sacred trees and holy wells, dedicated to their various gods. Christianity wisely simply rededicated them to the Virgin Mary or some renowned saint, and the pilgrims still come in their droves. Some pilgrimages are celebrated on annual feast days, called patterns.

There are five main pilgrimage trails—St Finbar's Pilgrim Path in Co Cork; >>

A roadside shrine outside Silvermines

This cross in Killaloe Cathedral came from Kilfinora

Pilgrim paths & sacred places

Holy Cross Abbey, Co Tipperary, in ruins for centuries, but now completely restored

The path to St Brigid's Shrine at Faughart, Co Louth

Holy wells are in roadside fields throughout Ireland

St Kevin's Way in Wicklow; Cnoch na d'Tobar and Cosán na Naomh, both in Co Kerry; and Tochar Pháraig in Mayo. A National Pilgrim-Paths Week is held annually at Easter time, and has been described as 'the Celtic Camino'.

Thousands of pilgrims climb Croagh Patrick—known as the Reek—on the last Sunday in July, honouring Saint Patrick, who is reputed to have fasted and prayed on the summit for forty days in the year 441. Of course the Druids wee bringing folks up there long before St Patrick.

There are also many holy wells and sacred shrines visited regularly by pilgrims, often praying for particular cures.

Famous is the ruined Benedictine Fore Abbey in Co Westmeath, which has seven wonders—built on a bog; a mill that ran without a headrace; water flowing uphill; a tree that won't burn; an anchorite buried in stone; a massive lintel stone lifted by St Féichín's prayer; and water that won't boil, but can cure ailments. And woe betide anyone who tries to boil it. ■

Fore Abbey, Co Westmeath, is famous for its 'Seven Wonders'

A holy well in a field in Co Clare

Pilgrims left these offerings

Clonmacnoise, Co Offaly, is a Mecca for pilgrims

Holy Island, Loch Derg

147

Co Wexford: Off Hook Head

Little roads by the sea

Sea road near Loop Head, Co Clare

The road by Galley Head, west Cork

WATER doesn't always have a good press. Perhaps with good reason—it sank the Titanic (well, ice did); it's dreary to drink; it creates tsunamis; it dilutes wine; it drowns people; worse still, it ruins a glass of whiskey. And it didn't do a whole lot for Noah.

Yet water is still the loveliest thing in the world to look at, especially when it's in an ocean. And one of the greatest blessings of living in this island of Ireland is that we so easily get to see the ocean, since so many of our roads >>

Near Tramore, Co Waterford

Co Louth: Road above Carlingford Loch

Road near Bantry

Little roads by the sea

Co Clare: Where the Burren meets the sea

Flags of many nations fly by the sea in east Cork

Valentia, Co Kerry

Achill Sound, Co Mayo

lead directly to the sea.

People have viewed the ocean from these roads since before history began. They did not always see beauty: they might have watched in terror as Viking dragon ships approached; or they might have been taking a last lingering look at their native harbour before descending to the pier where the coffin ship waited to take them away forever. Some of the sea roads go down to little long-deserted piers that flourished from the sea trade until larger ships demanded the bigger harbours of the great seaports. Some of those little piers, regrettably, are back in business again, to accommodate the smugglers of drugs.

We however can still look with joy from the little sea roads at the beauty that opens out before us. If we ever have the privilege to be with someone who is seeing the sea for the very first time, then we realise the wonder of it all.

The Wild Atlantic Way is a wonderful help to experiencing these sea roads, providing newsletters, maps, videos and advice. Just go to *wildatlanticway.com.* ■

Breezy morning at Inchidoney, Co Cork

Co Louth: Evening by the Dundalk-Carlingford road

Off Hook Head, Co Wexford

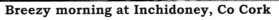

Coast road in north Clare

A field outside Newry, Co Down, with view of Carlingford Mountain (Slieve Foye)

Fields by the roadside

Tulip field in Co Offaly

View from Nenagh River walkway

Where sheep may safely graze—Co Clare

Silvermines, Co Tipperary

WHEN I was a child we used to go on lots of picnics. Our Dad and Mum would spread a couple of rugs on the grass, and we all sat on the rugs. No chairs or anything. There'd be sandwiches and a thermos flask of tea and maybe a few buns and a couple of apples. Nothing much really, but we children looked forward to those picnics. I always remember them as being in bright sunshine, and always in some lovely field just off the road.

We chose a different field every time. I think that's when I fell in love with >>

Fields by the roadside

We're learning to leave fields fallow for a while to help wildlife

Patchwork of fields by the sea in Co Cork

Grazing in Co Limerick

A field in east Clare

fields. Indeed I became a connoisseur of fields to picnic in. I particularly loved the ones with the gorse, blazing yellow with that coconut aroma in early spring. And maybe on a slope with a view over a river. Or alive with wild flowers. Or with a stream we could dam with stones and sods of earth. Or redolent of mown hay in autumn. I'm a bit unsure if we got permission to go into these fields—maybe farmers didn't much mind in those days, or maybe we just took a chance.

Fields are the little places of the earth. Places that no one knows except perhaps the farmer who works them, and where no one ever walks except that same farmer. Places that whirl past a railway-carriage window and are gone—seen by millions yet trodden by few. But often lovelier than any manicured Luxembourg Gardens or Hyde Park—lovely with that spontaneous beauty only rural nature can yield. And those fields are loved. If you want to know just how fierce that love can be, read John B. Keane's play, *The Field,* or watch the film. The love of a field can lead to murder.

The song sings of forty shade of green. I have counted them in our fields, and there are more.* ■

* Excerpted from *The Joy of Looking*

Knockanora hills in North Tipperary

Watch out for cattle before you go into a field

Early summer in this Kildare field

This is what we call the hungry grass of Ireland

Spring burning in Kerry

End of the road in east Cork

The end of the road

Ballyferriter, Co Kerry: Road ends with view of *An Fear Marbh* (The Dead Man)

Shannon floods at World's End, Castleconnell, Co Limerick

**Co Waterford:
This road leads into
the Comeragh Mountains
and just—stops!**

THE breakup of a relationship is one of the saddest of human experiences, and one of the saddest songs about it must be *End of the Road*, sung by Boys II Men. It's an apt title, for coming to the end of a road can at times indeed be sad.

But not always. There's another song from years ago, sung by Harry Lauder—*Keep Right on to the End of the Road*—which expresses hope for a happy ending: 'Where all the love you've been dreaming of / Will be there at the end of the road.' The only thing required >>

Inchidoney Island, Co Cork

The end of the road

Co Mayo: Not all roads end gently

Road to Martello tower near Ballyvaughan, Co Clare

Loch Owel, Co Westmeath

Near Cloughjordan

of us is determination never to quit.

Irish roads, like everything else in life (including this here book) have to come to an end. The ending can be abrupt and even dangerous, when the road ends at a cliff or an unguarded quay, and such endings have taken many a life.

At other times the end of a road can open onto a beautiful sparkling lake or a stunning vista of ocean and sky.

One of my greatest pleasures is to find myself on a little road for the first time, to put away map and compass, and wonder where the road will end.

Sometimes it just meets another road at a T-junction; other times a road stops in a field or a graveyard; or maybe just runs gently down to the sea. Didn't I tell you they're the roads to God-knows-where?

The fun is to explore them.

My ambition has long been to have explored every little road in Ireland before I die, but to do so I would have to live for at least another 300 years, which I think is rather unlikely.

The end of *my* road will come somewhat sooner.

By the way, thank you for reading to the end of this book. I really appreciate that. *Slán.* ∎

Road's end at Doonass Falls, Lower Shannon

End of the road near Bantry, Co Cork

Road ends at the lighthouse on Loop Head, Co Clare

Roads can end in a field

...or a graveyard by the sea

Drug-smuggler warning at cliff road, Dingle peninsula

Connemara seaside track

We're the end of your road...

159